F

Family Matters

The family is the true measure of the greatness of a nation,
just as the dignity of man is a true measure of civilization.

Pope John Paul II, Limerick, 1 October 1979.

Mark Hamilton

FOUR COURTS PRESS

Typesetting keyboarded by
Gilbert Gough Typesetting, Dublin
for Four Courts Press,
Kill Lane, Blackrock,
Co. Dublin.

A catalogue record for this book
is available from the British Library.

ISBN 1-85182-100-7

ACKNOWLEDGMENT
Publication of this book has been grant-aided
by the Dublin Diocesan Council for the Family.

Printed in the Channel Islands by
The Guernsey Press Ltd

Contents

For my parents
and for
Pat and Marie
Stephen and Marie
Sean and Jacinta

ONE

The value of the family

Until recently, the contribution of the family to the well-being of individuals and society has been largely undisputed. Now, along with other institutions, and perhaps more so, 'it has been beset by the many profound and rapid changes that have affected society and culture. Many families live through this situation remaining faithful to values that constitute the foundation of the institution of the family. Others have been uncertain and bewildered over their role or even doubtful and almost unaware of the ultimate meaning and truth of conjugal and family life. ... Others are hindered by various forms of injustice in the realization of their fundamental rights.'[1]*

In this chapter we will examine the contribution that the family can and does make to the individual and to society. We can then move on with conviction to outline a basis for achieving good family life.

PROBLEMS AND SOLUTIONS

1 If asked to list some of the problems facing society today, the following would likely appear on any concerned person's list:

*Most of the quotations in this book are drawn from the writings of Pope John Paul II. For simplicity and in order not to detract from the content of the points made, full details on the source of each quotation are given at the back of the book.

- increasing crime and vandalism
- materialistic outlook on life
- permissiveness
- drug abuse
- absenteeism
- alcohol abuse
- emigration, unemployment
- marriage breakdown
- abortion
- social inequality within society
- decline in moral standards.

Some of these problems are relatively new, others have roots in history. Some threaten individuals, others the family, others society. However, it would be wrong to throw one's hands in the air and to think that there are no solutions, for many solutions lie in *good family life*. It is for this reason that the Holy Father said in Kenya: 'The strength and vitality of any country will only be as great as the strength and vitality of the family within that country.'[2]

2 What has the family to offer to individuals and society? To answer this question it is useful to consider some distinctive characteristics of the family.

'The family, which is founded and given life by love, is a community of persons: of husband and wife, of parents and children, of relatives.'[3] It is a grouping which straddles generations.

Within the family there is a mutual sharing and a mutual acceptance of one person by another. 'A person is accepted for who he is rather than what he does.'[4] In the wider society the functional value of the person is more to the fore and a person is accepted on the basis of the contribution he can make to society. This unconditional acceptance which takes place within the family helps provide each person with the security he needs in order to develop and improve.

This mutual acceptance coupled with the continuity with past generations helps give a stability and permanence to values held within the family. It can therefore become, if the family so wishes, 'a school of virtue' for the young.

THE FAMILY HELPS SOCIETY

3 We can therefore highlight a number of ways in which the family can help its individual members:

- it provides security for all its members;
- it provides a common domicile where one is not always conscious of the need to perform for others;
- it provides education and training, especially for its younger members;
- it is a source of maintenance for its old and infirm members;
- it provides a home where one can experience the joy of knowing that one is loved simply for being oneself;
- it provides a climate in which one can develop one's own personality;
- it provides warmth and affection for all members and so helps in each person's emotional development; it provides a climate where one learns how to live, respecting others and appreciating their dignity;
- through the unconditional acceptance by its members of one another it encourages freedom and fosters independence;
- it can develop in each member a desire for personal improvement so as to be of greater service to others in the family and in society.

4 'Man cannot live without love. He remains a being that is incomprehensible to himself; for life is senseless if love is not revealed to him, if he does not encounter love, if he does not experience it and make it his own, if he does not participate intimately in it.'[5]

The family is a forum where this need can be realised—between husband and wife, between parents and children, between brothers and sisters, between relatives. . . .

5 Naturally, the personal advancement of individuals through the family results in the advancement of society as a whole.

Strong family life is characterised by a spirit of self-giving and service to others. In the family each member is called upon to consider others in any decision he might take—there is no absolute autonomy. Such attitudes in persons can help defeat self-centred individualism which serves only selfishness, and so guarantee a truly caring society.

'The family has vital and organic links with society, since it is its foundation and nourishes it continually through its role of service to life: it is from the family that citizens come to birth and it is within the family that they find the first school of the social virtues that are the animating principles of the existence and development of society itself.'[6]

6 'Consequently, faced with a society that is running the risk of becoming more and more depersonalised and standardised and therefore inhuman and dehumanizing, with the negative results of many forms of escapism—such as alcoholism, drugs and even terrorism—the family possesses and continues still to release formidable energies capable of taking man out of his anonymity, keeping him conscious of his personal dignity, enriching him with deep humanity and actively placing him, in his uniqueness and unrepeatability, within the fabric of society.'[7]

In short, the family gives each member a sense of identity which can be a springboard towards helping him shape a society which will serve mankind.

CAN THE FAMILY BE REPLACED?

7 Since the dawn of history as we know it, three thousand years before Christ, the institution of the family has been accepted as an irreplaceable constituent of civilization. Is it replaceable? Having considered how it serves individuals and society is it feasible to suggest that the family can be replaced? Russell Kirk,[8] a leading American thinker, certainly thinks not. The alternative to the family is the 'universal orphanage', a society of 'loveless individualism'. He points out that without the family the state will be required to substitute new compulsions where in the past willing co-operation had succeeded. The modern state, he claims, finds it difficult enough as it is to 'restrain the violent, educate the young, cheer the old and the sick and assure sustenance' without trying to take upon itself the work of the family.

TWO

Marriage — a most audacious contract

As a contract between two consenting adults, marriage is unrivalled in the depth and extent of the commitment involved. It is useful, and occasionally imperative, that a married couple would call to mind the extent to which they have given themselves to each other, so as to grow in their understanding of their commitment and see how they can draw more from it. We will now consider some aspects of this commitment.

WHAT IS MARRIAGE?

8 Marriage is the legitimate union between a man and a woman as husband and wife, binding them to a lifelong indivisible community of life. 'In marriage, the partners decide to give themselves to each other, realising that although external factors may change they themselves remain the same persons.'[1]

9 The natural institution of marriage, in being a loving union of husband and wife, serves as an image of the love that God has for his people. With the coming of Christ, his death and Resurrection, the natural institution of marriage was raised to a new level.

Jesus Christ sacrificed himself on the Cross for his Church

and thus the marriage of baptised persons becomes 'a real symbol of that new and eternal covenant sanctioned in the blood of Christ.'[2] It is this new meaning of marriage that we have in mind when we speak of *the sacrament of marriage.*

St Paul develops this idea very well when he says: 'That is why a man will leave his father and mother and will cling to his wife, and the two will become one flesh. Yes, these words are a high mystery, and I am applying them here to Christ and his Church.'[3]

10 'In the family there is the most admirable and close co-operation of man with God: the two human persons, created in the divine image and likeness, are called not only to the great task of continuing and prolonging the work of creation by giving physical life to new beings, in whom the life-giving Spirit infuses the mighty principle of immortal life, but also the nobler charge which perfects the first, of the civil and Christian education of their offspring.'[4] Owing to this essential characteristic Jesus willed that marriage be a *sacrament.*

THE POWER OF GRACE

11 A sacrament is a sensible and outward sign of inward grace, instituted by Jesus Christ.

The sacrament of marriage is therefore a channel of grace for the couple. 'It introduces Christ's love for the Church in the heart of the home.'[5] The sacrament gives supernatural aid (grace) to the couple to help them carry out their role in the family. All the commitments undertaken, will be backed up by this powerful supernatural resource. From here also arises all the help needed in difficulties. Grace acts as a 'stimulating impulse so that every day the couple may progress towards an ever richer union with each other on all levels—of the body, of the character, of the heart, of the intelligence and will, of the soul.'[6]

It thus makes sense that couples would *lean on* and *count on* the sacramental grace that is available to them.

12 'Hold high the esteem for the wonderful dignity and grace of the sacrament of marriage. Prepare earnestly for it. Believe in the spiritual power which the sacrament of Jesus Christ gives to strengthen the marriage union, and to overcome all the crises and problems of life together. Married people must believe in the power of the sacrament to make them holy; they must believe in their vocation to witness through their marriage to the power of Christ's love.'[7]

UNION AND COMMUNION

13 In God's plan 'marriage requires:

- *the faithful and permanent love* of husband and wife;
- *an indissoluble communion* that sinks its roots in the natural complementarity that exists between man and woman and is nurtured through the personal willingness of the spouses to share their entire life-project, what they have and what they are;
- *a community of persons* in which the love between husband and wife must be fully human, exclusive and open to new life.'[8]

14 'Christian spouses have promised to share with each other all they are and all they have. It is the most audacious contract that exists — and the most marvellous one.

The union of their bodies, willed by God himself as the expression of the even deeper communion of their minds and their hearts, carried out with equal respect and tenderness, renews the dynamism and the youth of their solemn commitment, of the first "yes".

The union of their characters: To love a person is to love him such as he is, it is to love him to the extent of cultivating in oneself the antidote of his weaknesses or his faults—for example, calm and patience, if the other manifestly lacks them.

The union of hearts: There are innumerable fine shades of difference between the love of man and that of woman. Neither of the partners can demand to be loved in the same way as he or she loves. It is important—on both sides—to renounce the secret reproaches that separate hearts and to free oneself of this sorrow at the most favourable moment. To share the joys, and, even more, the sufferings of the heart, is a strong bond of unity. But it is just as much in a shared love of the children that the union of hearts is strengthened.

The union of intelligences and wills: Spouses are two forces different but united for their mutual service, for the service of their home, their social environment and the service of God. Basic agreement must be worked out and shown in the determination and pursuit of a common purpose. The more energetic partner must support the will of the other, replace it sometimes, and act on it skillfully—in an instructive way—as a lever.

Finally, *the union of souls*: Each of the spouses must find time for moments of solitude with God, for heart-to-heart communication in which the partner is not the first concern. This indispensable personal life of the soul with God is far from excluding the sharing of all conjugal and family life. On the contrary it stimulates the Christian couple to look for God together, to discover his will together and to carry it out in practice with the light and the energies drawn from God himself.'[9]

INDISSOLUBLE

15 'By virtue of the sacramentality of their marriage, spouses are bound to one another in the most profoundly indissoluble manner.'[10]

16 'Through the power of the Holy Spirit, man and woman enter the marriage covenant between them which, by divine institution, "since the beginning" (cf. Genesis 2:24 and Matthew 19:5) is indissoluble. Rooted in the natural complementary nature of man and woman, indissolubility is sanctioned by the mutual promise of personal and total self-giving, and it is required for the good of the children.'[11]

This point echoes the message of Vatican II: 'as a mutual gift of two persons, this intimate union, as well as the good of the children, imposes total fidelity on the spouses and argues for an unbreakable oneness between them.'[12]

And as noted before the couple are not alone: 'a man and a woman . . . are assured of the help they need to develop their love in a faithful and indissoluble union, and to respond with generosity to the gift of parenthood.'[13] This is because through the sacrament of marriage, 'Christ himself becomes present in the life of the married couple and accompanies them.'[14]

17 For those who argue that 'it is too difficult, or indeed impossible, to be bound to one person for the whole of life',[15] it is necessary to explain that the personal and total self-giving *cannot* take place without the corresponding characteristic of indissolubility. No one can give himself or herself totally to the other without a guarantee that the relationship has a lifelong quality.

'What is of fundamental importance is that a person unites himself totally and forever, whatever may happen, to his husband or wife. He cuts out any possible retreat and is ready to share his future completely with another. From that moment on, the power and strength of God becomes present in the couple's love and helps them, because God himself is love, to complete self-giving.'[16]

CONSENT

18 'The marriage *consent* is an act of the will which signifies and involves a mutual giving which unites the spouses among themselves and at the same time binds them to the children which they may eventually have, with whom they constitute one family . . .'.[17] Such a commitment once made cannot be undone. It is not within the power of the spouse to take back what has been unconditionally given to the other. 'If one wishes the gift to be total it must be irrevocable and without reserve.'[18]

GIVING ALL

19 'Sexuality, by means of which man and woman give themselves to one another through the acts which are proper and exclusive to spouses, is by no means something purely biological, but concerns the innermost being of the human person as such. It is realized in a truly human way only if it is an integral part of the love by which a man and a woman commit themselves totally to one another until death.

The total physical self-giving would be a lie if it were not the sign and fruit of a total personal self-giving, in which the whole person, including the temporal dimension, is present: if the person were to withhold something or reserve the possibility of deciding otherwise in the future, by this very fact he or she would not be giving totally.'[19]

20 'Christ has freed man and woman for this possibility of loving each other in truth and fullness. The great danger for family life, in a society in which pleasure, comfort and independence are idols, lies in the fact that people may be induced to close their hearts to such a possibility, resigning themselves to a reduced ideal of married life. The Christian community must contest a view of the conjugal relationship which, instead of *unreserved mutual dedication*, proposes the mere co-existence of two loves, concerned, when all is said and done, only with themselves.'[20]

21 'By virtue of the covenant of married life, the man and woman "are no longer two but one flesh" (Matt 19:6) and they are called to grow continually in their communion through day-to-day fidelity to their marriage promise of total mutual self-giving. This conjugal communion sinks its roots in the natural complementarity that exists between man and woman, as it is nurtured through the personal willingness of the spouses to share their entire life-project, what they have and what they are.'[21]

The indissolubility of marriage is rooted in the personal and total self-giving of the couple. This self-giving will be practised continually throughout married life, replacing the cult of self-fulfilment which selfishness can promote. Before marriage, one could legitimately decide on many aspects of one's life without consulting others. Afterwards *dialogue* may well need to replace unilateral *decision.*

22 'To set out on the path of the married vocation means to *learn* married love day by day, year by year: love according to soul and body, love that is "patient, is kind, that does not insist on its own way . . . and does not rejoice at wrong": love that "rejoices in the right", love that "endures all things" (cf. St Paul's First Letter to the Corinthians, 13:4-7)'.[22]

Thus the marriage contract is an ongoing one, one which grows through self-giving — the measure of true love.

FREEDOM

23 There is a mistaken notion of freedom current today which has contributed to the difficulties facing some married couples.

Freedom is sometimes seen as an 'autonomous power of self-affirmation', an excuse always to put one's own well-being first, a right to do as one wishes. It is sometimes invoked as a reason for trying to take back in some way what one has freely given unconditionally.

If freedom is always closely allied with responsibility then there is a strong likelihood it will not be misunderstood. True freedom lies in living out God's plan, in being ready to bear the responsibility for one's actions.

THREE

A community of love and life

'Marriage is the beginning of the new community of love and life, on which man's future on earth depends.'[1]

True love is always associated with self-giving and this theme runs throughout the Church's teaching on sexual morality. The expression of love between spouses leads to a personification of that love each time they are blessed with another child.

SELF-GIVING VERSUS PRE-MARITAL SEX

24 'To love is, therefore, essentially to give oneself to others. Far from being an instinctive inclination, love is a conscious decision of the will to go towards others. To be able to love truly, it is necessary to detach oneself from many things and above all from oneself, to give gratuitously, to love to the end.'[2]

Such love, such self-giving, is the secret of commitment.

25 The natural and moral link between sexuality and marriage is challenged by a contemporary culture which trivialises sex, and consequently trivialises love. The New Testament teaches clearly that sex outside marriage is wrong, with many exhortations to chastity and purity. St Paul has this so say: 'Make no mistake about it; it is not the debauched, the idolators, adulterous, it is not the effeminate, the sinners against nature, the dishonest, the misers, the drunkards, the bitter of speech, the extortioners, that will inherit the kingdom of God.'[3]

26 In addressing the youth of Paris, the Pope reminded them of the reason why pre-marital sex is wrong: 'The union of bodies has always been the most forceful language in which two beings can communicate with each other. That is why this language, which touches the sacred mystery of man and woman, demands that the gesture of love should never be performed without the conditions of a complete and definitive assumption of responsibility for the partner, and that the commitment should be undertaken publicly in marriage.'[4]

27 Here we summarise a number of reasons why pre-marital sex is wrong.

'Total physical self-giving would be a lie if it were not the sign and fruit of a total personal self-giving, in which the whole person is present . . . the only "place" in which this self-giving in its whole truth is made possible is marriage.'[5]

There is an 'inseparable connection, established by God, which man on his own initiative may not break, between the unitive significance and the procreative significance which are both inherent to the marriage act'.[6] Thus the sexual act must always be open to life. Pre-marital sex shows *no* sense of responsibility with regard to future life.

The sexual urge is a very strong one. In a developing relationship it is important that mutual appreciation grow on all fronts. Because of its very power, sex tends to dominate if introduced into a relationship and so destroy its future fullness. The couple don't really know each other. They can become 'intoxicated by the sexual experience. When the boy makes sacrifices to be with the girl, she doesn't know why he made them. She doesn't know if he made them for love of her or for love of sex. The relationship is totally different from that of two people who are saving sex for marriage. Because of the false signals that it sets up, pre-marital sex leads to unwise marriages.'[7]

TRIAL MARRIAGES

28 The truth of genuine marriage cannot be honestly prepared for by the make-believe of a 'trial' marriage. 'Trial marriages, instead of being a preparation for successful marriage, are instead a psychological and moral preparation for instability in a future marriage. Having each experienced the other's readiness for one tentative "affair", a couple will find it more difficult to trust each other in a true marriage. They may even find it harder themselves to resist temptation to marital infidelity. There is no better foundation for trusting and trustworthy married love than for each partner to know that the other has had sexual relationships only with him or with her. Pre-marital chastity means being determined to keep the gift of oneself for the person one loves alone. It is manifestation of true love.'[8]

FEATURES OF MARRIED LOVE

29 Pope Paul VI in *Humanae Vitae* highlights the characteristic features of married love:

'This love is above all fully *human*, a compound of sense and spirit. It is not, then, merely a question of natural instinct or emotional drive. It is also, and above all, an act of the free will, whose dynamism ensures that not only does it endure through the joys and sorrows of daily life, but also that it grows, so that husband and wife become in a way one heart and one soul, and together attain their human fulfilment.

'Then it is a love which is *total*—that very special form of personal friendship in which husband and wife generously share everything, allowing no unreasonable exceptions or thinking just of their own interests. Whoever really loves his partner loves not only for what he receives, but loves that partner for her own sake, content to be able to enrich the other with the gift of himself.

'Again, married love is *truthful and exclusive* of all other, and this until death. This is how husband and wife understand it on the day on which, fully aware of what they were doing, they freely vowed themselves to one another in marriage. Though this fidelity of husband and wife sometimes presents difficulties, no one can assert that it is impossible, for it is always honourable and worthy of the highest esteem. The example of so many married persons down through the centuries shows not only that fidelity is connatural to marriage but also that it is the source of profound and enduring happiness.

'And finally this love is *creative of life*, for it is not exhausted by the loving interchange of husband and wife, but also contrives to go beyond this to bring new life into being. "Marriage and married love are by their character ordained to the procreation and bringing up of children. Children are the outstanding gift of marriage, and contribute in the highest degree to the parents' welfare".'[9]

30 'Conjugal love involves a totality, in which all the elements of the person enter—appeal to the body and instinct, power of feeling and objectivity, aspiration of the spirit and of will. It aims at a deeply personal unity, the unity that, beyond union in one flesh, leads to forming one heart and soul, it demands indissolubility and faithfulness in definitive mutual giving; and it is open to fertility.'[10]

31 'In its most profound reality, love is essentially a gift; and conjugal love, while leading the spouses to the reciprocal "knowledge" which makes them "one flesh", does not end with the couple, because it makes them capable of the greatest possible gift, the gift by which they become co- operators with God for giving life to a new human person. Thus the couple, while giving themselves to one another, give not just themselves but also the reality of children, who are a living reflection of their love . . .'.[11]

32 'While not making the other purposes of matrimony of less account, the true practice of conjugal love, and the whole meaning of family life which results from it, have this aim: that the couple be ready with stout hearts to co-operate with the love of the Creator and the Saviour, who through them will enlarge and enrich his own family day by day.'[12]

MARRIED LOVE IS OPEN TO CHILDREN

33 'Decisions about the number of children and the sacrifices to be made for them must not be taken only with a view to adding to comfort and preserving existence. Reflecting upon this matter before God, with the graces drawn from the Sacrament, and guided by the teachings of Church, parents will remind themselves that it is certainly less serious to deny their children certain comforts or material advantages then to deprive them of the presence of brothers and sisters, who could help them to grow in humanity and to realize the beauty of life at all its ages and in all its variety.'[13]

34 Speaking in Madrid in 1982, Pope John Paul II said: 'There is an unbreakable relationship between conjugal love and the transmission of life, in virtue of which, as Paul VI taught, "Every conjugal act must remain open to the transmission of life" (*Humanae Vitae*, 11) . . . I wrote in *Familiaris Consortio*, "The innate language that expresses the total reciprocal self-giving of husband and wife is overlaid, through contraception, by an objectively different language, namely, that of not giving oneself totally to the other. This leads not only to a positive refusal to be open to life but also to a falsification of the inner truth of conjugal love" (*Familiaris Consortio*, n. 32).'[14]

35 'It is only in the broad context of God's design for the family and for the creation of new life that one can consider the more specific question of the regulation of births. The wisdom of the Creator has enriched human sexuality with great values and a spiritual dignity. The vocation of Christian couples is to realize these values in their lives. . . .

'The design of the Creator has provided the human organism with structures and functions to assist couples in arriving at responsible parenthood. "In fact, as experience bears witness, not every conjugal act is followed by new life. God has wisely disposed natural laws and rhythms of fecundity which, of themselves, cause a separation in the succession of births" (*Humanae Vitae*, 11).

'Your task will never be reduced to a question of presenting one or other biological method, much less to any watering down of the challenging call of the infinite God. Rather your task is, in view of the situation of each couple, to see which method or combination of methods best helps them to respond as they ought to the demands of God's call.'[15]

GENEROSITY AND THE GIFT OF CHILDREN

36 At the present time many ideas which obscure truth and the dignity of the human person are widely promoted. Such ideas when backed up by powerful economic resources and actively promoted through the media tend to lessen man's capacity for objective judgment. The distortion of meaning of sexuality and the growing anti-life climate weaken man's commitment to objective moral standards. It is not surprising therefore that parents would find some aspects of the Church's teaching difficult to understand. If only one side of the story (for example, with regard to divorce or contraception) is continually promulgated through the means of social communication, then it can be difficult to come to terms with the true solutions to the problems facing the family today.

37 The separation of human sexuality from the person has resulted in distortion in understanding the task of transmitting life. In this context it is worth recalling that the teaching of the Church 'is founded upon the inseparable connection, willed by God and unable to be broken by man on his own initiative, between the two meanings of the conjugal act: the unitive meaning and the procreative meaning.'[16]

'Every action which, either in anticipation of the conjugal act, or in its accomplishment, or in the development of its natural consequences, proposes, whether as an end or as a means, to render procreation impossible'[17] must be excluded as intrinsically immoral.

Pope John Paul II develops this point further in *Familiaris Consortio*: 'When couples, by means of recourse to contraception, separate the two meanings that God the creator has inscribed in the being of man and woman and in the dynamism of their sexual communion they act as "arbiters" of the divine plan and they "manipulate" and degrade human sexuality—and with it themselves and their married partners —by altering its value of total self-giving. . . .

When, instead, by means of recourse to periods of infertility, the couple respect the inseparable connection between the unitive and procreative meanings of human sexuality, they are acting as "ministers" of God's plan and they "benefit from" their sexuality according to the original dynamism of "total" self-giving, without manipulation or alteration.'[18]

38 'The choice of the natural rhythms involves accepting the cycle of the person, that is the woman, and thereby accepting dialogue, reciprocal respect, shared responsibility and self-control. To accept the cycle and to enter into dialogue means to recognize both the spiritual and corporal character of conjugal communion, and to live personal love with its requirement of fidelity.'[19]

39 When addressing the Irish people in Limerick, Pope John Paul II stated: 'And here, I want to say a very special word to all Irish parents. Marriage must include openness to the gift of children. Generous openness to accept children from God as the gift of their love is the mark of the Christian couple. Respect the God-given cycle of life, for this respect is part of our respect for God himself, who created male and female, who created them in his own image, reflecting his own life-giving love in the patterns of their sexual being.'[20]

Married couples should not allow a consumerist mentality to lessen their generosity which is needed to raise new human life.

ABSTINENCE

40 Abstinence or periodic continence has an important role to play in marriage and helps to confer on conjugal love 'a higher human value. It demands continual effort, yet, thanks to its benificent influence, husband and wife fully develop their personalities, being enriched with spiritual values. Such discipline bestows upon family life fruits of serenity and peace, and facilitates the solution of other problems; it favours attention to one's partner, helps both parties to drive out selfishness, the enemy of true love, and deepen their sense of responsibility. By this means, parents acquire the capacity of having a deeper and more efficacious influence in the education of their offspring.'[21]

Married life often presents couples with opportunities to practice abstinence—for example: lack of privacy, separation from a spouse due to work, sickness or tiredness. It helps the spouses to grow in self-control and in their trust of one another.

41 The Church in its teaching on conjugal morality realises that 'sacrifice cannot be removed from family life, but must in fact be whole-heartedly accepted if the love between husband and wife is to be deepened and become a source of intimate joy.'[22]

RESPECT FOR NEW LIFE

42 *Certain fundamental values*, which cannot be violated without incalculable harm of a moral nature are bound up with the family. . . . Two such values fall into the context of conjugal love.

'The first of them is the value of the person which is expressed in absolute mutual faithfulness until death: the faithfulness of the husband to his wife and of the wife to her husband. The consequence of this affirmation of the value of the person, which is expressed in the mutual relationship between husband and wife, must also be respect for the personal value of the new life, that is, of the child, from the first moment of his conception.'[23]

43 'And so I say to all, have an absolute and holy respect for the sacredness of human life from the first moment of its conception. Abortion, as the Vatican Council stated, is one of the "abominable crimes" (*The Church in the Modern World*, 51). To attack unborn life at any moment from its conception is to undermine the whole moral order which is the true guardian of the well-being of man. The defence of the absolute inviolability of unborn life is part of the defence of human rights and human dignity.'[24]

44 'I am speaking of the absolute respect for human life which no person or institution, private or public, can ignore. Therefore, whoever denies protection to the most innocent and weakest human person, to the human person already conceived even though not yet born, would commit a most serious violation of the moral order. The killing of an innocent child is never legitimate. Such would undermine the very foundation of society.

'What sense would there be in speaking of the dignity of man, of his fundamental rights, if an innocent human being is not protected, or even if the point is reached of providing means or services, private or public, for the destruction of defenceless human lives?'[25]

45 'The family is placed at the very centre of the common good in its various dimensions precisely because man is conceived and born in it. Everything possible must be done in order that this human being should be desired, awaited and experienced as a particular, unique and unrepeatable value, right from the beginning, from the moment of his conception. He must feel that he is important, useful, dear and of great value, even if infirm or handicapped; even more loved, in fact, for this reason.'[26]

STERILITY

46 Procreation is not always possible, but conjugal life does not lose its value on account of this. The absence of children should be an occasion for couples to live a wider spirit of service to society.

'Physical sterility in fact can be for spouses the occasion for other important services to the life of the human being, for example, adoption, various forms of educational work, and assistance to other families and to the poor or handicapped chidren.'[27]

LOVE WITHIN THE FAMILY

47 'The family, which is founded and given life by love, is a community of persons; of husband and wife, of parents and children, of relatives . . . without love the family cannot live, grow and perfect itself as a community of persons.'[28]

All members of the family have the responsibility of building up this community—a task which requires a spirit of service and self-giving, a 'sharing of goods, of joys and of sorrows'.[29]

48 'The fundamental form of life and love within the family lies in respect for each person, for each individual member of the family. Husbands and wives, consider and treat each other with the greatest respect. Parents, respect the unique personality of your children. Children, show your parents obedient respect. All members of the family must feel accepted, and respected, because they feel loved. In a special way, the old and the sick.

'Respect in its deepest sense means fidelity. Respect means acceptance of one another, trust and attachment, patience and forgiveness when necessary, beyond and in spite of personal difficulties, which can never justify a lack of love.'[30]

49 'Christian couples must not forget that the secret of married happiness lies in everyday things, not in daydreams. It lies in finding the hidden joy of coming home in the evening; in affectionate relations with their children; in everyday work in which the whole family co-operates; in good humour in the face of difficulties that should be met with a sporting spirit; in making the best use of all the advances that civilization offers to help us bring up children, to make the home pleasant and life more simple.

'I constantly tell those who have been called by God to form a home to love one another always, to love each other with the love of their youth. Anyone who thinks that love ends when the worries and difficulties that life brings with it begin, has a poor ideal of marriage, which is a sacrament and an ideal and a vocation. It is precisely then that love grows strong. Torrents of worries and difficulties are incapable of drowning true love because people who sacrifice themselves generously together are brought closer by their sacrifice.'[31]

THE EXTENDED FAMILY

50 The elderly have to be fully integrated into the circle of family life.

'There are cultures which manifest a unique veneration and great love for the elderly. They continue to be present and to take an active and responsible part in family life, through having to respect the autonomy of the new family; above all they carry out the important mission of being a witness to the past and a source of wisdom for the young and for the future. Other cultures, however, especially in the wake of disordered industrial and urban development, have both in the past and in the present set the elderly aside in unacceptable ways. This causes acute suffering to them and spiritually impoverishes many families.'[32]

51 'When a society, allowing itself to be guided solely by the criteria of consumption and efficiency, divides people into active and inactive and considers the mature as second-class citizens, abandoning them to loneliness, it cannot be called a truly civilized society. When a family does not wish to have in the house their own blood relatives, the very young and the elderly, children and old people, and one neglects the other in some way or manner, it certainly does not deserve to be called a loving community.'[33]

52 'Living with their flesh and blood, the elderly can, with the appropriateness and the discretion that this will always require, bring to their relatives the benefit of that affection and wisdom, that understanding and indulgence, of advice and comfort, of faith and prayer, which are for the most part, the charisms of the twilight of life.'[34]

FOUR

Parents — first and primary educators

New life brings new responsibilities and the joys of a growing family are coupled with the difficulties of educating children in a changing society, unsure of its directions. The tensions that can exist between family life and life in the wider environment are numerous. How can the Christian family cope?

RESPONSIBILITIES IN EDUCATION

53 'Since parents have conferred life on their children, they have a most solemn obligation to educate their offspring. Hence, parents must be acknowledged as the first and foremost educators of their children. Their role as educators is so decisive that scarcely anything can compensate for their failure in it. For it devolves on parents to create a family atmosphere so animated with love and reverence for God and others that a well rounded personal and social development will be fostered among the children. Hence, the family is the first school of those social virtues which every society needs.'[1]

Parental love 'enriches the education of the children with the values of kindness, constancy, goodness, service, disinterestedness and self-sacrifice.'[2]

54 'In education, the child must find the possibilities of developing in a healthy, normal way on the physical, intellectual, moral, spiritual and social plane, in conditions of freedom and dignity.'[3]

55 With so many conflicting ideas in the outside world, the difficulties facing parents in the education of their children are many and varied. However, they have the grace of the Sacrament of marriage to help them. 'It enriches them with wisdom, counsel, fortitude and all the other gifts of the Holy Spirit in order to help the children in their growth as human beings and as Christians.'[4] 'Nothing is more important than to be a good Christian father and mother.'[5]

BEING PARENTS

56 '*All members* of the family, each according to his or her own gift, have the grace and responsibility of building, day by day, the communion of persons, making the family a "school of deeper humanity": this happens where there is care for the little ones, the sick, the aged; where there is mutual service every day; when there is a sharing of goods, of joys and of sorrows.'[6] Pope John XXIII highlighted two aspects of the educational work of parents. To mothers he said: 'The mother's voice, when it encourages, invites, beseeches, remains carved in the depths of her children's hearts, and is never forgotten. Oh, only God knows the good done by this voice, and its services to the Church and to human society.'[7] And to fathers: 'In families in which the father prays and has a joyful and conscious faith, attends catechetical instructions and takes his children there, there will not be storms and desolations of a rebellious and enstranged youth. Our word wishes to be always one of hope, but we are certain that, in some discouraging expressions of youthful life, the greatest responsibility lies with the fathers of families, who shirk the precise and serious duties of their state.'[8]

57 For parents, the children are more important than business, work, bridge, golf or rest. Parents, especially fathers, should realise this and so should want to be with the children, spending time with them—in homework, in sports, in listening to them. This attitude will facilitate parents' friendship with their children and thus make the task of education so much easier.

'The ideal attitude of parents lies more in becoming their children's friends—riends who will be willing to share their anxieties, who will listen to their problems, who will help them in an effective and agreeable way.'[9]

58 Children learn from the example rather than the 'preaching' of their parents. The unconscious good example of parents becomes the ideal of the child.

In *God and Children*, a spiritual book for parents, the following advice is given to fathers: 'You teach much more when you are not trying to teach, than when you put on a serious face and frown and set out to give lessons. When you come home from work, when you leave down the newspaper to talk to them, when you are having meals with them, when you pray, when you get down on your hands and knees and play with them, when you smile with your lips but your eyes show that you are worried about something, when you do not boast nor look for compliments, when you refuse to be downhearted by others' jealousy, then, when you are least concerned with teaching your children, they think to themselves: I want to be like my father.'[10]

59 However, despite the importance of example in education, advice also needs to be given, and sometimes very clearly. Parents cannot afford to neglect this responsibility.

Parents take for granted that their child knows right from wrong and assume that the child has the moral character to always do what is right. Given the prevailing moral climate such parents can only be described as naive. It is necessary to explain what is right conduct in many different ways and to encourage the child in Christian virtue. Parents should be ready to listen, to debate, to explain and to be demanding on their children, particularly during their teenage years.

'In their conversations, parents should make an effort to listen, to pay attention, to understand, to recognise the fact that their children are sometimes partly right—or even completely right—in some of their rebellious attitudes. At the same time, they should help their children to direct their efforts and to carry out their projects properly, teaching them to consider things and to reason them out. It is not a matter of imposing a line of conduct, but rather of showing the human and supernatural motives for it. In a word, parents have to respect their children's freedom, because there is no real education without personal responsibility, and there is no responsibility without freedom.'[11]

60 'Children and young people should be helped to develop harmoniously their physical, moral and intellectual qualities. They should be trained to acquire gradually a more perfect sense of responsibility in the proper development of their own lives by constant effort and in the pursuit of liberty, overcoming obstacles with unwavering courage and perseverance. As they grow older they should receive a positive and prudent education in matters relating to sex. Moreover, they should be so prepared to take their part in the life of society that, having duly trained in the necessary and useful skills, they may be able to participate actively in the life of society in its various aspects. They should be open to dialogue with others and should willingly devote themselves to the promotion of the common good.'[12]

61 A number of characteristics of punishment could be highlighted—punishment which will help a child to acquire the habit of responsibility. 'Punishment should be given calmly, tactfully, opportunely, clearly, reasonably, without trying to humiliate, without being absurd, to the degree of sending a boy of twelve to his room for the whole of a Sunday afternoon.'[13]

A punishment should be related to the action done and proportionate to the fault. It should *not* be administered in anger and after its administration the offence should be forgotten.

62 'It is up to parents to introduce children into educative communities wider than the family. The latter must then accompany its adolescents, with patient love, in hope, and, *without resigning its task*, co-operating with other educators. In this way, strengthened in their Chrisitan identity to face in the right way a pluralistic world, often indifferent or even hostile to their convictions, these young people will be able to become strong in faith, serve society, and take an active part in the life of the Church.'[14]

No matter what barriers may develop between parents and their children during the teenage years, if there is good effort put into understanding, while knowing how to be firm, then family life will be enhanced.

TEACHING MORALITY

63 Children and adolescents must be helped 'to make sound moral judgments and to put them into practice with a sense of personal commitment, and to know and love God more perfectly.'[15]

64 'The education of the moral conscience, which makes every human being capable of judging and of discerning the proper ways to achieve self-realization, according to his or her original truth, thus becomes a pressing requirement that cannot be renounced.'[16]

For young people to follow their conscience they first of all need an understanding of what is right and what is wrong. They may not always have the reasons worked out fully—that can come later—but parents should ensure that, as a minimum, the principles are put clearly to their children.

Schools should also support parents in this moral education, and parents should ensure that the moral education programmes in schools are firmly based on Christian principles. Many programmes available (even in Catholic schools) do not fulfil this criteria as they draw on secular humanistic psychology, and so can do untold damage in deforming the conscience of the young.

65 Parents must educate their children in 'the essential values of human life'.

'Children must grow up with a *correct attitude of freedom with regard to material goods*, by adopting a simple and austere life style and being fully convinced that "man is more precious for what he is than for what he has".'[17] 'Children must be enriched not only with a *sense of true justice*, which alone leads to respect for the personal dignity of each individual, but also, and more powerfully, by a *sense of true love*, understood as sincere solicitude and disinterested service with regard to others, especially the poorest and those in most need.'[18]

SEX EDUCATION

66 'Faced with a culture that largely reduces human sexuality to the level of something commonplace, . . . by linking it solely with the body and with selfish pleasure, the educational service of parents must aim firmly at a training in the area of sex that is truly and fully personal: for sexuality is an enrichment of the whole person—body, emotions and soul—and it manifests its inmost meaning in leading the person to the gift of self in love.'[19]

67 'Sex education, which is a basic right of parents, must always be carried out under their attentive guidance, whether at home or in educational centres chosen and controlled by them.'[20]

68 'The task of forming young people's standards in the matter of purity is a particular responsibility of parents. It should be parents who teach their children gradually about the origins of life, in accordance with their mentality and capacity to understand, gently anticipating their natural curiosity. This is very important. There is no reason why children should associate sex with something sinful or find out about something that is in itself noble and holy in a vulgar conversation with a friend. This can also be an important step in strengthening the friendship between parents and children, preventing a separation in the early moments of their moral life.'[21]

Be aware that there are many other sources, sources which will mis-inform unless you inform.

69 'If they do not ask where babies come from, then go ahead and tell them unasked. . . . Tell them where babies come from, and I promise you it will give them a great love for their mother, a great respect for womanhood and a holy pride in themselves. There is no need to wait until they are fourteen to tell them the father's function, and they will then begin to appreciate, naturally and supernaturally, the spark of creative power God has given to man.

'The young girl should know the cause of menstruation and its relation to the sacred duty of motherhood. She should know—because you should explain it to her—that her early maturity accounts for the attraction she feels for boys who are older than she is.

'The young boy should be told the cause of those involuntary emissions which he will have at night, and how that function, which should be used exclusively within marriage, plays its part in bringing new lives into the world.'[22]

To give sex education to their children, parents need to explain things simply and early, to speak more about purity than impurity, to get across the idea of reverence for this God-given gift, to help it to be seen in the context of love (which is always self-sacrificing). If such positive sex education is omitted, there is a real danger that misinformation will replace information. There is no real substitute for sex education under the caring guidance of parents if they want their child to have a fully balanced understanding of its creative power.

70 'Listen to your children. Give them your time, even the time that you have reserved for yourselves. Show them your confidence; believe whatever they tell you, even if sometimes they try to deceive you. Don't be afraid when they rebel, because, at their age, you yourselves were more or less rebellious. Go to meet them half-way and pray for them. If you act in this Christian manner, they will come to you with simplicity, instead of trying to satisfy their legitimate curiosity by taking it to some rough or vulgar friend. Your confidence, your friendly dealings with your children, will receive an answer in their sincerity in dealing with you.'[23]

ROLE OF GRANDPARENTS

71 In the matter of education, parents should consider the enormous potential of the elderly.

'The various generations come together and help one another to grow wiser and to harmonise personal rights with the other requirements of social living.'[24] 'The elderly often have the charism to bridge generation gaps before they are made: how many children have found understanding and love in the eyes and words and caresses of the aging.'[25]

MEDIA EDUCATION

72 Nowadays, members of the family are often widely separated from each other for the greater part of the day. This factor, allows the mass-media: papers, cinema, radio, television and video recorders, play a big part in the lives of most families.

Parents must be aware of the dangers that this situation can present and 'ensure that the use of the media in the family is carefully regulated. Families should also take care to seek for their children other forms of entertainment that are more wholesome, useful and physically, morally and spiritually formative "*to develop and use to advantage the free time of the young and direct their energies*".'[26]

73 Parents have to ensure that their children form their consciences according to Christian values and not according to erroneous standards which may be set by public opinion or mass media.

This can be achieved by

(a) *Vigilance* 'The vision furnished to them by the media often differs profoundly from that which the family would wish to transmit to them. Parents, in many cases, do not show sufficient concern about this. Generally they pay vigilant attention to the types of friends with whom their children associate, but do not exercise a similar vigilance regarding the ideas which the radio, the television, records, papers and comics carry into the "protected" and "safe" intimacy of their homes. And so the mass media often enter the lives of the youngest members of the family with no possibility of the necessary explanations or corrections from parents or other educators which could neutralise any harmful elements.'[27]

(b) *Critical faculties* 'They must take a more searching look at the content of programmes offered to them. They must exercise judgment on the messages which the media are transmitting to them.'[28]

(c) *Getting involved with media* 'Parents will endeavour to influence the selection and preparation of the programmes themselves, by keeping contact—through suitable initiatives—with those in charge of the various phases of production and transmission. In this way they will ensure that the fundamental values that form part of the true good of society are not ignored or deliberately attacked.'[29]

A CIVILISING INFLUENCE

74 Part of the education the family provides is the experience of living together with others. At times, this can make demands on one or many in the family, demands which can lead to disagreement and discord.

'Family communion can only be preserved and perfected through a great spirit of sacrifice. It requires, in fact, a ready and generous openness of each and all to understanding, to forbearance, to pardon, to reconciliation. There is no family that does not know how selfishness, discord, tension and conflict violently attack and at times mortally wound its own communion: hence there arises the many and varied forms of division in family life. But, at the same time, every family is called by the God of peace to have the joyous and renewing experience of "reconciliation".'[30]

75 'In the family are born these fundamental relations of brotherhood, which constitute the very basis of social brotherhood thanks to which men communicate with one another as true brothers, who walk together along the way of life, not as competitors, strangers or even enemies, but helping one another to reach their highest goals.'[31]

A MODEL FOR ALL FAMILIES

76 'I end by putting before all families for imitation, and for help in their family life, the Holy Family of Nazareth. It was in this family that the Son of God spent his childhood and grew to manhood. It is the model of all Christian families.'[32]

FIVE

The domestic church

'The home should be the first school of religion, as it must be the first school of prayer.'[1] In preparing children for the life ahead of them, parents will also consider how to prepare them for the afterlife. Handing on the faith in the home assumes a great importance in the education of children in this increasingly irreligious world.

EDUCATING IN THE FAITH

77 Regarding Christian education, Vatican II says the following: 'Such an education does not merely strive to foster maturity in the human person. Rather, its principal aims are these: that as baptised persons are gradually introduced into a knowledge of the mystery of salvation, they may daily *grow more conscious of the gift of faith* which they have received; that they may *learn to adore* God the Father in spirit and in truth, especially *through liturgical worship*; that they may be trained to *conduct their personal life in true righteousness and holiness*, according to their own nature, and thus grow in maturity, to the statute of the fulness of Christ, and devote themselves to the upbuilding of the Mystical Body. Moreover, aware of their calling, they should *grow accustomed to giving witness* to the hope that is in them and to promoting Christian transformation of the world.'[2]

78 'When they become parents, spouses receive from God the gift of a new responsibility. Their parental love is called to become for the children the visible sign of the very love of God.'[3]

Educating in the faith is thus a very natural task for truly loving parents. 'The domestic faith, the quality and holiness of the family, the education of your children, depend on the observance of your (marriage) commitments.'[4]

BAPTISM

79 'In the family the human person is not only brought into being and progressively introduced by means of education into the human community, but by means of the rebirth of baptism and education in the faith the child is also introduced into God's family, which is the Church.'[5]

Baptism introduces the child into a new life, a life in the Christian family. He needs to be educated in this new life.

80 By Baptism, a person becomes a child of God and heir to the kingdom of heaven. Because of its importance it is recommended that Baptism should not be postponed unnecessarily without serious cause.

FAMILY PRAYER

81 'Parents are the first catechists of their children. . . . In this catechetical activity, prayer should have the place of honour.'[6] Through prayer, parents initiate their children into the search for God. The Pope also reminded the Irish people at Limerick that 'your homes should always remain homes of prayer.'[7]

82 'Mothers, do you teach your children the Christian prayers? Do you prepare them, in conjunction with the priests, for the sacraments that they receive when they are young: Confession, Communion and Confirmation? Do you encourage them when they are sick to think of Christ suffering, to invoke the aid of the Blessed Virgin and the Saints? Do you say the family Rosary together? And you, fathers, do you pray with your children, with the whole domestic community, at least sometimes? Your example of honesty in thought and action, joined to some common prayers, is a lesson for life, and act of worship of singular value.'[8]

83 'Apart from morning and evening prayers, certain forms of prayer are to be expressly encouraged, . . . such as reading and meditating on the word of God, preparation for the reception of the sacraments, devotion and consecration to the Sacred Heart of Jesus, the various forms of veneration of the Blessed Virgin Mary, grace before and after meals, and observance of popular devotions.'[9]

84 'While respecting the freedom of the children of God, the Church has always proposed certain practices of piety to the faithful with particular solicitude and insistence. Among these should be mentioned the recitation of the Rosary: "We now desire, as a continuation of the thought of our predecessors, to recommend strongly the recitation of the family Rosary. . . . There is no doubt that . . . the Rosary should be considered as one of the best and most efficacious prayers in common that the Christian family is invited to recite"[10].'[11]

85 'To say the Holy Rosary, considering the mysteries, repeating the Our Father and Hail Mary, with the praises to the Blessed Trinity and the constant invocation of the Mother of God, is a continuous act of faith, hope and love, of adoration and reparation.'[12]

LITURGY AND FAMILY OCCASIONS

86 'An important purpose of the prayer of the domestic church is to serve as the natural introduction for the children to the liturgical prayer of the whole Church, both in the sense of preparing for it and of extending it into personal, family and social life. Hence the need for gradual participation by all the members of the Christian family in the celebration of the Eucharist, especially on Sundays and feastdays, and of the other sacraments, particularly the sacraments of Christian initiation of the children.'[13]

If a couple can manage to bring the younger children to Mass then this can be very worthwhile. Explanations can be given gradually as to what is taking place in the Mass and children thus learn to grow in piety and in reverence for the House of God.

87 'Joys and sorrows, hopes and disappointments, births and birthday celebrations, wedding anniversaries of the parents, departures, separations and homecomings, important and far-reaching decisions, the death of those who are dear, etc.—all of these mark God's loving intervention in the family's history. They should be suitable moments for thanksgiving, for petition, for trusting abandonment of the family into the hands of the common Father in heaven.'[14]

88 'Catechesis is more incisive when, in the course of family events (such as the reception of the sacraments, the celebration of great liturgical feasts, the birth of a child, a bereavement) care is taken to explain in the home the Christian or religious content of these events. But that is not enough: Christian parents must strive to follow and repeat, within the setting of family life, the more methodical teaching received elsewhere.'[15]

Some celebration of feastdays (for example, some special dish or menu for dinner to mark the day) can help make the family aware of their importance and provide an opportunity of explaining the occasion or meaning behind each of them.

89 'All Soul's Day is a special day for families. On this day they make their way to the places where their closest and dearest departed ones rest; they meet, in silence, in prayer, in meditation, at their tombs.

'They relive joyful and sorrowful memories, sometimes the tears begin to stream down their cheeks, so great is the sense of nearness, in spite of death; so great is the emotion!

'Those who have passed away also belong to the family; they remain in hearts, because the mystery of life and love has bound them so deeply to them. They live on in their widowers or widows who are still alive. They live on in their children, left orphans . . .'.[16]

HANDING ON THE FAITH

90 'In places where anti-religious legislation endeavours to prevent education in the faith, and in places where widespread unbelief or invasive secularism makes real religious growth practically impossible, "the Church of the home" remains the one place where children and young people can receive an authentic catechesis.'[17]

In such circumstances a great obligation befalls parents to educate their children at home. Such education should be structured, perhaps by following a textbook or basic catechetical text, so as to ensure it is thorough.

91 'The family must educate the children for life in such a way that each one may fully perform his or her role according to the vocation received from God. Indeed, the family that is open to transcendent values, that serves its brothers and sisters with joy, that fulfils its duties with generous fidelity, and is aware of its daily sharing in the mystery of the glorious Cross of Christ, becomes the primary and most excellent seedbed of vocations to a life of consecration to the Kingdom of God.'[18]

92 'There is perhaps no better model for a Christian couple than that of the Christian families of apostolic times: the centurion Cornelius, who obeyed the will of God and in whose home the Church was made accessible to the Gentiles; Aquila and Priscilla, who spread Christianity in Corinth and Ephesus, and who co-operated in the apostolate of St Paul; Tabitha, who out of charity attended the needs of the Christians in Joppe. And so many other homes of families of Jews and Gentiles, Greeks and Romans, in which the preaching of our Lord's first disciples began to bear fruit. Families who lived in union with Christ and made him known to others.'[19]

93 'The family of Nazareth . . . really constitutes that culminating point of reference for the holiness of every human family. The history of this family is described very concisely in the pages of the Gospel. We get to know only a few events in its life. However, what we learn is sufficient to be able to invoke the fundamental moments in the life of every family, and to show that dimension to which all men who live a family life are called: fathers, mothers, parents, children. The Gospel shows us, very clearly, the educative aspect of the family. "He went down with them and came to Nazareth, and was obedient to them" (Luke 2:51).'[20]

94 'The Holy Family of Jesus, Mary and Joseph is a model of life for every man, for every Christian, for every family community. . . . Just as the Holy Family of Nazareth was a very special place of love, the truly exceptional atmosphere in which there reigned mutual respect for each individual person and for his vocation, and also the first school in which the Christian message was loved intensely, so the Christian and human family is, and must be, a community of love and life; for these are its fundamental values.'[21]

SIX

Society serving the family

The family as a society ordained to the good of the individual person and to the good of human kind has fundamental natural rights deserving of protection. Society is called upon to respect, defend and promote these rights.

HELP FROM THE STATE

95 'The family and society have complementary functions in defending and fostering the good of each and every human being. But society—more specifically the State—must recognise that "the family is a society in its own original right" and so the State is under a grave obligation in its relations with the family to adhere to the principle of subsidiarity.

By virtue of this principle, the State cannot and must not take away from families the functions that they can just as well perform on their own or in free associations; instead it must positively favour and encourage as far as possible responsible initiative by families. In the conviction that the good of the family is an indispensable and essential value of the civil community, the public authorities must do everything possible to ensure that families have all those aids—economic, social, educational, political and cultural assistance—that they need in order to face all their responsibilities in a human way.'[1]

Thus the State must have a real willingness to place itself at the service of the family.

96 Marital stress and marriage breakdown can be attributed to a wide variety of causes, many of which are a consequence of economic and social factors. *For example*:

- increased industrialisation accompanied by population movement into cities and towns;
- break-up of close knit communities due to housing policies;
- increased mobility because of unemployment difficulties;
- financial worries due to high mortgage payments and high taxation;
- financial structures that make it almost a requirement that both parents work outside the home;
- job insecurity.

The State must do all in its power to help lessen the damaging impact of these difficulties.

The Church exhorts all men to see 'that in social administration, consideration is given to the requirements of families in the matter of housing, education of children, working conditions, social security and taxes; and that in regulations governing emigration, family life is perfectly safeguarded.'[2]

HELP FROM THE CHURCH

97 'One of the chief duties of the Church is to protect the institution of the family, building it on the principles of the Christian faith, giving suitable preparation to the spouses together with the constant help of the sacraments and the moral support of the community, and by educating them for a life of love, fidelity and patience, and by introducing the custom of family prayers.'[3]

98 In 1983 the Holy See presented a Charter of the Rights of the Family.

This Charter is a formulation of the fundamental rights that are inherent in the family, 'rights which arise in the ultimate analysis, from that law which is inscribed by the Creator in the heart of every human being.

'Society is called upon to defend these rights against all violations and to respect and promote them in the entirety of their content.'[4]

This Charter is reproduced in the Appendix (pp. 67-76).

PRE-MARRIAGE TRAINING

99 Society and the Church should be involved in the effort of properly preparing young people for the future responsibilities of married life. In this way the couple will be better able to face the problems that can confront them.

Long term preparation takes place within the family: 'It is the period when esteem for all authentic human values is instilled, both in interpersonal and in social relationships, with all that this signifies for the formation of character, for the control and right use of one's inclinations, for the manner of regarding and meeting people of the opposite sex, and so on. Also necessary, especially for Christians, is the solid spiritual and catechetical formation that will show that marriage is a true vocation and mission, without excluding the possibility of the total gift of self to God in the vocation to the priestly or religious life.'[5]

Proximate preparation through pre-marriage courses should include the following topics:

- explanation of the sacramental aspects of marriage;
- marriage as an interpersonal relationship;
- nature of conjugal sexuality and responsible parenthood (with the essential medical and biological knowlege connected with it);
- methods for the education of children;
- administration of financial and housekeeping resources;
- preparation for a family apostolate.

HELP FROM THE SCHOOL

100 Parents seeking to educate their children are faced with a number of difficulties:

- the requirements of education go far beyond the capabilities and qualifications of the family, because of the vast accumulation of knowledge;
- parents can have too little time to spend with their children because of the demands of their employment;
- a generation gap exists which in some countries is ever-widening due to the pace of development;
- children are becoming independent of their parents at an increasingly early age;
- the communications media has a pervasive influence on children from an early age.

So, parents need, and usually expect, the support of the school in the all-round education of their children. The school's responsibility is to complement the work of the parents.

101 'The right of parents to choose an education in conformity with their religious faith must be absolutely guaranteed.

'The State and the Church have the obligation to give families all possible aid to enable them to perform their educational role properly.

'. . . Those in society who are in charge of schools must never forget that the parents have been appointed by God himself as the first and principal educators of their children and that their right is completely inalienable.'[6]

SEX EDUCATION IN SCHOOLS

102 '. . . the present trend in education in human sexuality. One does not need a doctorate in psychology to know that everything related to human sexuality is extremely provocative to adolescent boys and girls. This reaction has been given by the Creator to procure the survival of the human race. But God has endowed the young with a natural modesty, which is reinforced in a good home, to protect them from misusing their generative powers until they are old enough to use them legitimately and provide for the education and support of the children God may send them. If a school or other educational centre presumes to teach sexuality in a manner that is contrary to the moral common sense of parents, that strips away the instinctive, healthy, personal modesty with which God endows youth, that suggests explicitly or by calculated omission that there is no right or wrong in any sexual conduct if enough individuals practise it, and that offers the same young people instruction on mechanical contraception and abortion as a remedy for sexual indulgence, then parents have not only the right but the duty to stand up and defend ethical sanity and Christian morality.'[7]

WOMEN AND WORK

103 Social planning and policy in modern society has left many women with little choice in the question of whether they work outside the home.

'In a world that is becoming ever more sensitive to women's rights, what is to be said of the rights of women who want to be or need to be full-time wives and mothers? Are they to be burdened by a taxation system that discriminates against women who choose not to leave the home in order to earn a separate income? Without infringing the freedom of anyone to seek fulfilment in employment and activities outside the home, should not the work of the homemaker too be properly appreciated and adequately supported?'[8]

104 'There must be a social re-evaluation of the mother's role, of the toil connected with it, and of the need that children have for care, love and affection in order that they may develop into responsible, morally and religiously mature and psychologically stable persons. It will rebound to the credit of society to make it possible for a mother—without inhibiting her freedom, with psychological or practical discrimination, and without penalizing her as compared with other women—to devote herself to taking care of her children and educating them in accordance with their needs, which vary with age. Having to abandon their tasks in order to take up paid work outside the home is wrong from the point of view of the good of society and of the family when it contradicts or hinders these primary goals of the mission of a mother. . . .

'The true advancement of labour requires that labour should be structured in such a way that women do not have to pay for the advancement by abandoning what is specific to them and at the expense of the family, in which women as mothers have an irreplaceable role.'[9]

105 A hectic urban life, demanding long hours of work from a father or mother, can be disruptive of family life.

'Work, therefore cannot destroy the family: on the contrary it must unite it, help it to perfect its cohesion. *The rights of the family must be deeply inscribed in the very foundations of every code of work*, since the latter has as its subject man, and not just production and profit. How, for example, can a satisfactory solution be found for the problem — similar in many countries — of the woman who works in a factory, at a tiring pace, and who is constantly concerned about being with her children and her husband?'[10]

SEVEN

Renewing society through the family

As families become more aware of the problems presented by a world society which seems to be losing its sense of God, they begin to wonder what the future holds. Families themselves hold the key. Family life lived well can be a powerful antidote to the world's problems and can bring about a renewal of society.

BATTLES TO BE FOUGHT

106 In considering negative aspects of the situation of the family in the world today, Pope John Paul II highlighted the following points:

'Signs are not lacking of a degradation of some fundamental values: a mistaken theoretical and practical concept of the independence of the spouses in relation to each other, serious misconceptions regarding the relationships of authority between parents and children; the concrete difficulties that the family itself experiences in the transmission of values; the growing number of divorces; the scourge of abortion; the ever more frequent recourse to sterilisation; the appearance of a truly contraceptive mentality.

'At the root of these negative phenomena there frequently lies a corruption of the idea and experience of freedom, conceived not as a capacity for realizing the truth of God's plan for marriage and the family, but as an autonomous power of self-affirmation, often against others, for one's own selfish well-being.'[1]

Such considerations help one to see where renewal is needed in society and to realise that renewal depends largely on the family.

107 'When we speak of the right to life, to physical and moral integrity, to nourishment, to housing, to education, to health care, to employment, to shared responsibility in the life of the nation, we speak of the human person. It is this human person whom faith makes us recognise as created in the image of God and destined for an eternal goal. The family apostolate must watch over the defence of these rights.'[2]

FIGHTING FOR LIFE AND HUMAN HAPPINESS

108 'We will stand up every time that human life is threatened. When the sacredness of life before birth is attacked, we will stand up and proclaim that no one ever has the authority to destroy unborn life. When a child is described as a burden or is looked upon only as a means to satisfy an emotional need, we will stand up and insist that every child is a unique and unrepeatable gift of God, with the right to a loving and united family. When the institution of marriage is abandoned to human selfishness or reduced to a temporary, conditional arrangement that can easily be terminated, we will stand up and affirm the indissolubility of the marriage bond. When the value of the family is threatened because of social and economic pressures, we will stand up and reaffirm that the family is "necessary not only for the private good of every person, but also for the common good of every society, nation and state". When freedom is used to dominate the weak, to squander natural resources and energy, and to deny basic necessities to people, we will stand up and re-affirm the demands of justice and social love. When the sick, the aged or the dying are abandoned in loneliness, we will stand up and proclaim that they are worthy of love, care and respect.'[3]

THE FAMILY'S RESOURCES

109 'It is necessary to restore confidence to Christian families. In the storm now raging over it, under indictment as it is, the Christian family is more and more tempted to give way to discouragement, lack of confidence in itself, and fear. We must, therefore, tell it, with true and convincing words, that it has a mission and a place in the modern world, and that, to carry out this task, it has formidable resources and lasting values.

'These values are above all of a spiritual and religious order: there is a sacrament at the root and at the base of the family, a sacrament which is a sign of the active presence of the Risen Christ within the family, just as it is also an inexhaustible source of grace.

'But these values are also of a natural order. . . . These values are love, faithfulness, mutual help, indissolubility, fecundity in its fullest meaning, intimacy enriched by opening towards others, the awareness of being the original cell of society, etc.'[4]

With such strengths, Christian families can contribute 'to giving back to the present-day world the zest for life.'[5]

110 'I am thinking, dear brothers and sisters, of the contribution that Christian families, well formed and exemplary as regards morals can make to the proclamation of the Gospel. . . . Even where Christian families are only a tiny minority in the midst of an environment that is mainly non-Christian, the witness they bear to other families is indispensable and extremely precious. If they are deeply imbued with the proclamation of the Gospel, they will have the same effectiveness as that yeast which, hidden in three measures of flour, makes the whole mass ferment (Mt 13:33).'[6]

In short, '*future evangelisation* depends largely on the domestic Church.'[7]

A CHRISTIAN APOSTOLATE

111 'The family is a way of speaking about God with others'.[8]

112 The extent of the apostolate of the Christian family is outlined in *The Christian Family in the Modern World:*

'This apostolate will be exercised in the first place within the families of those concerned, through the witness of a life lived in conformity with the divine law in all its aspects, through the Christian formation of the children, through helping them to mature in faith, through education in chastity, through preparation for life, through vigilance in protecting them from the ideological and moral dangers with which they are often threatened, through their gradual and responsible inclusion in the ecclesial community and the civil community, through help and advice in choosing a vocation, through mutual help among family members for human and Christian growth together, and so on. The apostolate of the family will also become wider through words of *spiritual and material charity* towards other families, especially those most in need of help and support, towards the poor, the sick, the old, the handicapped, orphans, widows, spouses that have been abandoned, unmarried mothers and mothers-to-be in difficult situations who are tempted to have recourse to abortion, and so on.'[9]

BEARING WITNESS TO LIFE AND TO MARRIAGE

113 'It is necessary to re-awaken in consciences the sense of the sacredness of the life of every human being, at every stage of his existence.'[10]

114 'To bear witness to the inestimable value of the indissolubility and fidelity of marriage is one of the most precious and most urgent tasks of Christian couples in our time.'[11]

AN APOSTOLATE OF EXAMPLE

115 'Families will share their spiritual riches generously with other families too. . . . This the family will do by the mutual love of the spouses, by their generous fruitfulness, their solidarity and faithfulness, and by the loving way in which all the members of the family work together.'[12]

116 'The cult of purity is the most precious honour and treasure of the Christian family.'[13]

117 'A form of missionary activity can be exercised even within the family. This happens when some member of the family does not have the faith or does not practice it with consistency. In such a case the other members must give him or her a living witness of their own faith in order to encourage and support him or her along the path towards full acceptance of Christ the Saviour. . . .

'The Church of the home is also called to be a luminous

sign of the presence of Christ and of his love for those who are "far away", for families who do not yet believe and for those Christian families who no longer live in accordance with the faith that they once received.'[14]

FAMILY MEMBERS SERVING SOCIETY

118 'The great forces which shape the world—politics, the mass media, science, technology, culture, education, industry and work—are precisely the areas where lay people are especially competent to exercise their mission. If these forces are guided by people who are true disciples of Christ, and who are, at the same time, fully competent in the relevant secular knowledge and skill, then indeed will the world be transformed from within by Christ's redeeming power.'[15]

The family should strive to develop among its members this apostolic ambition—to place Christ at the centre of all human activities.

119 'Another task for the family is to form persons in love and also to practise love in all its relationships, so that it does not live closed in on itself, but remains open to the community, moved by a sense of justice and concern for others, as well as by a consciousness of its responsibility towards the whole of society.'[16]

120 'Young married couples should learn to accept willingly, and make good use of, the discreet, tactful and generous help offered by other couples that already have more experience of married and family life. . . . Thus there will take place a mutual exchange of presence and help among all the families, each one putting at the service of the others its own experience of life, as well as the gifts of faith and grace.'[17]

121 'Christian families will be able to show greater readiness to adopt and foster children who have lost their parents or have been abandoned by them. Rediscovering the warmth of affection of a family, these children will be able to experience God's loving and provident fatherhood witnessed to by Christian parents, and they will thus be able to grow up with generosity and confidence in life.'[18]

ON THE MARGINS OF SOCIETY

122 'Families, either singly or in association, can and should devote themselves to manifold social service activities, especially in favour of the poor, or at any rate for the benefit of all people and situations that cannot be reached by the public authorities' welfare organisation.'[19]

A family should seek to involve all its members in such activities, which are always available. In every neighbourhood there are persons who are old, poor or lonely who would appreciate a visit, a helping hand or words of encouragement.

123 'A vast field of activity lies open to families: today, even more preoccupying than child abandonment is the phenomenon of social and cultural exclusion, which seriously affects the elderly, the sick, the disabled, drug addicts, ex-prisoners, etc.'[20]

SUPPORT FOR THOSE SEPARATED

124 'Loneliness and other difficulties are often the lot of separated spouses, especially when they are the innocent parties. The ecclesial community must support such people more than ever. It must give them much respect, solidarity, understanding and practical help, so that they can preserve their fidelity even in their difficult situation; and it must help them to cultivate the need to forgive which is inherent in Christian love, and to be ready perhaps to return to their former married life.'[21]

SUPPORTING MOTHERHOOD

125 'The mother who is about to give birth cannot be left alone with her doubts, difficulties and temptations. We must stand by her side, so that she will not put a burden on her conscience, so that the most fundamental bond of man's respect for man will not be destroyed. Such, in fact, is the bond that begins at the moment of conception, as a result of which we must all, in a certain way, be with every mother who must give birth; and we must offer her all the help possible.'[22]

FAMILY POLITICS

126 'The social role of families is called upon to find expression also in the form of political intervention: families should be the first to take steps to see that the laws and institutions of the State not only do not offend, but support and positively defend the rights and duties of the family. Along these lines, families should grow in awareness of being "protagonists" of what is known as "family politics" and assume responsibility for transforming society; otherwise families will be the first victims of the evils that they have done no more than note with indifference.'[23]

Families should seek to ensure that the law aims at upholding that which is good, on the understanding that the law can generate a peer pressure on members of society. If something is sanctioned in law it implies that it is approved by society and is morally acceptable. World experience over the past thirty years has shown that only positive action by families in 'family politics' can ensure that State laws will defend and support the rights of the family.

THE HOLY FAMILY AS A PROTOTYPE

127 The Holy Family is 'the prototype and example for all Christian families. It was unique in the world. Its life was passed in anonymity and silence in a little town in Palestine. It underwent trials of poverty, persecution and exile. It glorified God in an incomparably exalted and pure way. And it will not fail to help Christian families—indeed, all the families in the world—to be faithful to their day-to-day duties, to bear the cares and tribulations of life, to be open and generous to the needs of others, and to fulfil with joy the plan of God in their regard.'[24]

The Charter of the Rights of the Family

The Charter of the Rights of the Family was drawn up by the Holy See in October 1983 so as to identify the fundamental rights inherent in the family.

The Charter is addressed principally to governments. In reaffirming, for the good of society, the common awareness of the essential rights of the family, the Charter offers to all who share responsibility for the common good a model and a point of reference for the drawing up of legislation and family policy, and guidance for action programmes.

At the same time the Holy See confidently proposes this document to the attention of intergovernmental international organisations which, in their competence and care for the defence and promotion of human rights, cannot ignore or permit violations of the fundamental rights of the family.

The Charter is of course also directed to the families themselves: it aims at reinforcing among families an awareness of the irreplaceable role and position of the family; it wishes to inspire families to unite in the defence and promotion of their rights; it encourages families to fulfil their duties in such a way that the role of the family will become more clearly appreciated and recognised in today's world.

The Charter is directed, finally, to all men and women, and especially to Christians, that they will commit themselves to do everything possible to ensure that the rights of the family are protected and that the family institution is strengthened for the good of all mankind, today and in the future.

Preamble

Considering that:

A. the rights of the person, even though they are expressed as rights of the individual, have a fundamental social dimension which finds an innate and vital expression in the family;

B. the family is based on marriage, that intimate union of life in complementary between a man and a woman which is constituted in the freely contracted and publicly expressed indissoluble bond of matrimony, and is open to the transmission of life;

C. marriage is the natural institution to which the mission of transmitting life is exclusively entrusted;

D. the family, a natural society, exists prior to the State or any other community, and possesses inherent rights which are inalienable;

E. the family constitutes, much more than a mere juridical, social and economic unit, a community of love and solidarity, which is uniquely suited to teach and transmit cultural, ethical, social, spiritual and religious values, essential for the development and well-being of its own members and of society;

F. the family is the place where different generations come together and help one another to grow in human wisdom and to harmonise the rights of individuals with other demands of social life;

G. the family and society, which are mutually linked by vital and organic bonds, have a complementary funtion in the defence and advancement of the good of every person and of humanity;

H. the experience of different cultures throughout history has shown the need for society to recognise and defend the institution of the family;

I. society, and in a particular manner the State and International Organisations, must protect the family through measures of a political, economic, social and juridical character, which aim at consolidating the unity and stability of the family so that it can exercise its specific function;

J. the rights, the fundamental needs, the well-being and the values of the family, even though they are progressively safeguarded in some cases, are often ignored and not rarely undermined by laws, institutions and socio-economic programmes;

K. many families are forced to live in situations of poverty which prevent them from carrying out their role with dignity;

L. the Catholic Church, aware that the good of the person, of society and of the Church herself passes by way of the family, has always held it part of her mission to proclaim to all the plan of God instilled in human nature concerning marriage and the family, to promote these two institutions and to defend them against all those who attack them;

M. the Synod of Bishops celebrated in 1980 explicitly recommended that a Charter of the Rights of the Family be drawn up and circulated to all concerned;

the Holy See, having consulted the Bishops' Conferences, now presents this

CHARTER OF THE RIGHTS OF THE FAMILY

and urges all States, International Organizations, and all interested Institutions and persons to promote respect for these rights, and to secure their effective recognition and observance.

Article 1
All persons have the right to the free choice of their state of life and thus to marry and establish a family or to remain single.

a) Every man and every woman, having reached marriage age and having the necessary capacity, has the right to marry and establish a family without any discrimination whatsoever; legal restrictions to the exercise of this right, whether they be of a permanent or temporary nature, can be introduced only when they are required by grave and objective demands of the institution of marriage itself and its social and public significance; they must respect in all cases the dignity and the fundamental rights of the person.

b) Those who wish to marry and establish a family have the right to expect from society the moral, educational, social and economic conditions which will enable them to exercise their right to marry in all maturity and responsibility.

c) The institutional value of marriage should be upheld by the public authorities; the situation of non-married couples must not be placed on the same level as marriage duly contracted.

Article 2
Marriage cannot be contracted except by the free and full consent of the spouses duly expressed.

a) With due respect for the traditional role of the families in certain cultures in guiding the decision of their children, all pressure which would impede the choice of a specific person as spouse is to be avoided.

b) The future spouses have the right to their religious liberty. Therefore to impose as a prior condition for marriage a denial of faith or a profession of faith which is contrary to conscience, constitutes a violation of this right.

c) The spouses, in the natural complementarity, which exists between man and woman, enjoy the same dignity and equal rights regarding the marriage.

Article 3

The spouses have the inalienable right to found a family and to decide on the spacing of births and the number of children to be born, taking into full consideration their duties towards themselves, their children already born, the family and society, in a just hierarchy of values and in accordance with the objective moral order which excludes recourse to contraception, sterilization and abortion.

a) The activities of public authorities and private organisations which attempt in any way to limit the freedom of couples in deciding about their children constitute a grave offence against human dignity and justice.

b) In international relations, economic aid for the advancement of peoples must not be conditioned on acceptance of programmes of contraception, sterilisation or abortion.

c) The family has a right to assistance by society in the bearing and rearing of children. Those married couples who have a large family have a right to adequate aid and should not be subjected to discrimination.

Article 4

Human life must be respected and protected absolutely from the moment of conception.

a) Abortion is a direct violation of the fundamental right to life of the human being.

b) Respect for the dignity of the human being excludes all experimental manipulation or exploitation of the human embryo.

c) All interventions on the genetic heritage of the human

person that are not aimed at correcting anomalies constitute a violation of the right to bodily integrity and contradict the good of the family.

d) Children, both before and after birth, have the rights to special protection and assistance, as do their mothers during pregnancy and for a reasonable period of time after childbirth.

e) All children, whether born in or out of wedlock, enjoy the same right to social protection, with a view to their integral personal development.

f) Orphans or children who are deprived of the assistance of their parents or guardians must receive particular protection on the part of society. The State, with regard to foster-care or adoption, must provide legislation which assists suitable families to welcome into their home children who are in need of permanent or temporary care. This legislation must, at the same time, respect the natural rights of the parents.

g) Children who are handicapped have the right to find in the home and the school an environmental suitable to their human development.

Article 5

Since they have conferred life on their children, parents have the original, primary and inalienable right to educate them; hence they must be acknowledged as the first and foremost educators of their children.

a) Parents have the right to educate their children in conformity with their moral and religious convictions, taking into account the cultural traditions of the family which favour the good and the dignity of the child; they should also receive from society the necessary aid and assistance to perform their educational role properly.

b) Parents have the right to choose freely schools or other means necessary to educate their children in keeping with their convictions. Public authorities must ensure that public subsidies are so allocated that parents are truly free to exercise this right without incurring unjust burdens. Parents should not have to sustain, directly or indirectly, extra charges which would deny or unjustly limit the exercise of this freedom.

c) Parents have the right to ensure that their children are not compelled to attend classes which are not in agreement with their own moral and religious convictions. In particular, sex education is a basic right of the parents and must always be carried out under their close supervision, whether at home or in educational centres chosen and controlled by them.

d) The rights of parents are violated when a compulsory system of education is imposed by the State from which all religious formation is excluded.

e) The primary right of parents to educate their children must be upheld in all forms of collaboration between parents, teachers and school authorities, and particularly in forms of participation designed to given citizens a voice in the functioning of schools and in the formulation and implementation of educational policies.

f) The family has the right to expect that the means of social communication will be positive instruments for the building up of society, and will reinforce the fundamental values of the family. At the same time the family has the right to be adequately protected, especially with regard to its youngest members, from the negative effects and misuses of the mass media.

Article 6

The family has the right to exist and to progress as a family.

a) Public authorities must respect and foster the dignity, lawful independence, privacy, integrity and stability of every family.

b) Divorce attacks the very institution of marriage and of the family.

c) The extended family system, where it exists, should be held in esteem and helped to carry out better its traditional role of solidarity and mutual assistance, while at the same time respecting the rights of the nuclear family and the personal dignity of each member.

Article 7

Every family has the right to live freely in its own domestic religious life under the guidance of the parents, as well as the right to profess publicly and to propagate the faith, to take part in public worship and in freely chosen programmes of religious instruction, without suffering discrimation.

Article 8

The family has the right to exercise its social and political function in the construction of society.

a) Families have the right to form associations with other families and institutions, in order to fulfil the family's role suitably and effectively, as well as to protect the rights, foster the good and represent the interests of the family.

b) On the economic, social, juridical and cultural levels, the rightful role of families and family associations must be recognized in the planning and development of programmes which touch on family life.

Article 9

Families have the right to be able to rely on an adequate family policy on the part of public authorities in the juridical, economic, social and fiscal domains, without any discrimination whatsoever.

a) Families have the right to economic conditions which

assure them a standard of living appropriate to their dignity and full development. They should not be impeded from acquiring and maintaining private possessions which would favour stable family life; the laws concerning inheritance or transmission of property must respect the needs and rights of family members.

b) Families have the right to measures in the social domain which taken into account their needs, especially in the event of the premature death of one or both parents, of the abandonment of one of the spouses, of accident, of sickness or invalidity, in the case of unemployment, or whenever the family has to bear extra burdens on behalf of its members for reasons of old age, physical or mental handicaps or the education of children.

c) The elderly have the right to find within their own family or, when this is not possible, in suitable institutions, an environment which will enable them to live their later years of life in serenity while pursuing those activities which are compatible with their age and which enable them to participate in social life.

d) The rights and necessities of the family, and especially the value of family unity, must be taken into consideration in penal legislation and policy, in such a way that a detainee remains in contact with his or her family and that the family is adequately sustained during the period of detention.

Article 10

Families have a right to a social and economic order in which the organisation of work permits the members to live together, and does not hinder the unity, well-being, health and the stability of the family, while offering also the possibility of wholesome recreation.

a) Remuneration of work must be sufficient for establishing and maintaining a family with dignity, ctiher through a suitable salary, called a 'family wage', or through other social measures such as family allowances or the remuneration of the work in the home or one of the parents; it should be such that mothers will not be obliged to work outside the home to the detriment of family life and especially of the education of the children.

b) The work of the mother in the home must be recognised and respected because of its value for the family and for society.

Article 11

The family has the right to decent housing, fitting for family life and commensurate to the number of the members, in a physical environment that provides the basic services for the life of the family and the community.

Article 12

The families of migrants have the right to the same protection as that accorded other families.

a) The families of immigrants have the right to respect for their own culture and to receive support and assistance towards their integration into the community to which they contribute.

b) Emigrant workers have the right to see their family united as soon as possible.

c) Refugees have the right to the assistance of public authorities and International Organizations in facilitating the reunion of their families.

Notes

Chapter 1: **The value of the family**

1. John Paul II, Apostolic Exhortation on the Christian Family in the Modern World, *Familiaris Consortio* (henceforth *FC*), 2 (1981). **2.** Ibid., Homily in Nairobi, Kenya, 7 May 1980. **3.** *FC*, 18. **4.** David Isaacs, *Character Building*, Dublin (1984). **5.** John Paul II, Encyclical Letter, *Redemptor Hominis*, 10 (1979). **6.** *FC*, 42. **7.** *FC*, 43. **8.** Russell Kirk in *Position Paper* 125, Dublin (1984).

Chapter 2: **Marriage: a most audacious contract**

1. Hamilton, M. & Logan, D., *The Case Against Divorce—60 Reasons for saying No*, Dublin (1986). **2.** *FC*, 13. **3.** St Paul, *Letter to the Ephesians*, 5:31-33. **4.** John XXIII, *Discorsi*, Vol. XX. **5.** Bishop Kevin McNamara, *The Family Today*, Dublin (1984). **6.** *FC*, 19. **7.** John Paul II, Homily in Limerick, Ireland, 1 October 1979. **8.** Ibid., Homily in Perth, Australia, 30 November 1986. **9.** Ibid., Homily in Kinshasha, Zaire, 3 May 1980. **10.** *FC*, 13. **11.** Ibid., Homily in Braga, Portugal, 15 May 1982. **12.** Vatican II, *Gaudium et Spes*, 48. **13.** John Paul II, Homily in Washington, USA, 7 October 1979. **14.** Ibid. **15.** *FC*, 20. **16.** Cardinal Franz Koenig, Pastoral Letter on the Family, 1978. **17.** John Paul II, Address to the Roman Rota, 28 January 1982. **18.** Ibid. **19.** *Familiaris Consortio*, 11. **20.** John Paul II, Address to a family advisory group, 29 November 1980. **21.** *FC*, 19. **22.** John Paul II, Apostolic Letter to World Youth, 1985.

Chapter 3: **A community of love and life**

1. John Paul II, Homily in Rome, Italy, 20 January 1980. **2.** Ibid., Homily to the Youth of Paris, France, 1 June 1980. **3.** St Paul, *First Letter to the Corinthians*, 6:10. **4.** John Paul II, Homily to the Youth of Paris, France, 1 June 1980. **5.** *FC*, 1. **6.** Paul VI, Encyclical Letter on the Regulation of Birth, *Humanae Vitae*, 12. **7.** Marshall Fightlin, "A Catholic Understanding of Marital Intimacy" in *New Oxford Review*, 1984. **8.** Irish Bishops' Lenten Pastoral, *Love is for Life*, 80, 1985. **9.** Paul VI, *Humanae Vitae*, 9. **10.** *FC*, 13. **11.** *FC*, 14. **12.** Vatican II, *Gaudium et Spes*, 50. **13.** John Paul II, Homily in Washington, USA, 7 October 1979. **14.** Ibid., Homily in Madrid, Spain, 2 November 1982. **15.** Ibid., Address to Family Congress of Africa and Europe, 15 January 1981. **16.** Paul VI, *Humanae Vitae*, 4. **17.** Ibid., 14. **18.** *FC*, 32. **19.** *FC*, 32. **20.** John Paul II, Homily in Limerick, Ireland, 1 October 1979. **21.** Paul VI, *Humanae Vitae*, 21. **22.** *FC*, 34. **23.** John Paul II, Homily in Rome, 31 December 1978. **24.** Ibid., Homily in Limerick, Ireland, 1 October 1979. **25.** Ibid., Homily in Madrid, Spain, 2 November 1982. **26.** Ibid., Audience in Rome, 3 January 1979. **27.** *FC*, 14. **28.** *FC*, 18. **29.** *FC*, 21. **30.** John Paul II, Homily in Onitsha, Nigeria, 13 February 1982. **31.** Ven. Josemaría Escrivá, "Women in social life and in the life of the Church" in *Conversations with Mgr. Escrivá*, Shannon (1968). **32.** *FC*, 27. **33.** John Paul II, Address to Federation of Elderly, Rome, 29 April 1982. **34.** Ibid., Message to World Assembly on Aging, 22 July 1982.

Chapter 4: **Parents: first and primary educators**

1. Vatican II, *Gravissimum Educationis*, 3. **2.** *FC*, 36. **3.** UN Declaration of the Rights of the Child. **4.** *FC*, 38. **5.** John Paul II, Homily in Limerick, Ireland, 1 October 1979. **6.** *FC*, 21. **7.** Ibid., *Discorsi*, Vol. II, p. 67. **8.** John XXIII, *Discorsi*, Vol. IV, p. 272. **9.** Ven. Josemaría Escrivá, "Marriage a Christian Vocation" in *Christ is Passing By*, Dublin (1974). **10.** J. Urteaga, *God and*

Children, Dublin (1965). **11.** Ven. Josemaría Escrivá, "Marriage a Christian Vocation" in *Christ is Passing By*, Dublin (1974). **12.** Vatican II, *Gravissimum Educationis*, 1. **13.** J. Urteaga, *God and Children*, Dublin (1965). **14.** John Paul II, Homily to Family Congress, Rome, 30 October 1978. **15.** Vatican II, *Gravissimus Educationis*, 1. **16.** *FC*, 8. **17.** Vatican II, *Gaudium et Spes*, 35. **18.** *FC*, 37. **19.** *FC*, 37. **20.** *FC*, 37. **21.** *Conversations with Mgr. Escrivá*, 100, Shannon (1968). **22.** J. Urteaga, *God and Children*, Dublin (1965). **23.** Ven. Josemaría Escrivá, "Marriage a Christian Vocation" in *Christ is Passing By*, Dublin (1974). **24.** Vatican II, *Gaudium et Spes*, 52. **25.** John Paul II, Homily to Forum on Aging, Rome, September 1980. **26.** *FC*, 76. **27.** John Paul II, Message for World Communications Day, 1980. **28.** Ibid. **29.** *FC*, 76. **30.** *FC*, 30. **31.** John Paul II, Address to Family Congress, Rome, 7 December 1981. **32.** Bishop Kevin McNamara, *The Family Today*, Dublin (1984).

Chapter 5: **The domestic church**

1. John Paul II, Homily in Limerick, Ireland, 1 October 1979. **2.** Vatican II, *Gravissimum Educationis*, 2. **3.** *FC*, 14. **4.** John Paul II, Homily in Rome, 3 December 1978. **5.** *FC*, 15. **6.** John Paul II, Message for World Mission Day, June 1981. **7.** Ibid., Homily in Limerick, Ireland, 1 October 1979. **8.** Paul VI, Address in Rome, 11 August 1976. **9.** *FC*, 61. **10.** Paul VI, Apostolic Exhortation, *Marialis Cultus*, 52 (1974). **11.** *FC*, 61. **12.** Ven. Josémaría Escrivá, *Holy Rosary*, Dublin (1974). **13.** *FC*, 61. **14.** *FC*, 59. **15.** John Paul II, Apostolic Exhortation, *Catechesi Tradendae*, 1979. **16.** Ibid., Address in Rome, 2 November 1980. **17.** *Catechesi Tradendae*, 1979. **18.** *FC*, 53. **19.** Ven. Josemaría Escrivá, "Marriage a Christian Vocation" in *Christ is Passing By*, Dublin (1974). **20.** John Paul II, Homily in Rome, 31 December 1978. **21.** Ibid., Address in Rome, 28 December 1980.

Chapter 6: **Society serving the family**

1. *FC*, 45. **2.** Vatican II, *Apostolicam Actuositatem*, 11. **3.** John Paul II, Address to Hungarian Bishops, October 1982. **4.** The Charter of the Rights of the Family, Rome, October 1983. **5.** *FC*, 66. **6.** *FC*, 40. **7.** Cardinal Oddi, Address to Congress of Catholics United for the Faith, July 1983. **8.** John Paul II, Homily in Perth, Australia, 30 November 1986. **9.** Ibid., Encyclical Letter, *Laborem Exercens*, 1981. **10.** Ibid., Homily at St Denis, Paris, 31 May 1980.

Chapter 7: **Renewing society through the family**

1. *FC*, 6. **2.** John Paul II, Address to Argentine Bishops, October 1979. **3.** Ibid., Homily in Washington, USA, 7 October 1979. **4.** Ibid., Address to Synod Fathers, 12 October 1980. **5.** Ibid., Address to families, Rome, 10 November 1980. **6.** Ibid., Address in Rome, 16 October 1981. **7.** *FC*, 65. **8.** Film, "The Divine Paths of the Earth", Italian TV Network 1979. **9.** *FC*, 71. **10.** John Paul II, Address in Rome, 21 December 1981. **11.** *FC*, 20. **12.** *FC*, 50. **13.** John XXIII, *Discorsi*, Vol. X, 1959. **14.** *FC*, 54. **15.** John Paul II, Homily in Limerick, Ireland, 1 October 1979. **16.** Synod of Bishops, Message to Christian Families, October 1980. **17.** *FC*, 69. **18.** *FC*, 41. **19.** *FC*, 44. **20.** *FC*, 41. **21.** *FC*, 83. **22.** John Paul II, Address in Rome, 3 January 1979. **23.** *FC*, 44. **24.** *FC*, 86.